WHERE WE LIVE

BOA EDITIONS, LTD.:
NEW POETS OF AMERICA SERIES

WHERE WE LIVE
Poems by
PETER MAKUCK

Foreword by Louis Simpson

BOA EDITIONS, LTD. • BROCKPORT NEW YORK • 1982

Grateful acknowledgement is made to the editors of the following publications in which these poems or earlier versions of them originally appeared:

The Beloit Poetry Journal: "Meat," "Back Roads by Night"; *The Carleton Miscellany:* "Lapidary"; *Chicago Review:* "Skating"; *Cimarron Review:* "Teachers"; *Denver Quarterly:* "Dépaysé II"; *The Greensboro Review:* "Where We Live"; *The Hudson Review:* "Sleds on the Rue de L'Eglise," "Above Challes-les-Eaux," "To the Snow-walker," "Letter Poem"; *Illinois Quarterly:* "Steel Valley"; *The Davidson Miscellany:* "Deliverance"; *Mid-American Review:* "Christmas at North Mountain," "Along the Phoenix Canals"; *Mississippi Review:* "The Split"; *The Nation:* "Dépaysé I"; *New River Review:* "Nights"; *North American Review:* "A Walkabout"; *The Ohio Review:* "Holding On"; *Ploughshares:* "Players," "Rerun Scene: You Rescue My Son"; *Poetry Now:* "Racing"; *Porch:* "Southern Snow"; *Prairie Schooner:* "Wine Country Near Les Abymes"; *Southern Poetry Review:* "Hunger," "Pitt County, North Carolina"; *The Southern Review:* "Dziadek," "The Commons"; *Tar River Poetry:* "Driving to Youngstown," "Witness"; *Wisconsin Review:* "My Son Draws an Apple Tree."

Designed and printed at the Visual Studies Workshop, Rochester, N.Y.
Typeset by Open Studio, Rhinebeck, N.Y.
Cover photograph by Robert Bretz.

Publication of this book was made possible with the assistance of a grant from the Literature Program of The New York State Council on the Arts.

ISBN 0-918526-40-X Cloth
      0-918526-41-8 Paper
Library of Congress #82-071633

First Edition: November 1982

BOA Editions, Ltd.
A. Poulin, Jr., Publisher
92 Park Avenue
Brockport, N.Y. 14420

for my mother and father, givers

Contents

Foreword by Louis Simpson

I

II

III

Foreword

A poet said that we want the poet to build us his world. This is what Peter Makuck has done. It begins with memory; an uncle gave you the binoculars he used at the battle of Midway. He carved your name in the shell of a turtle and told you that some live to be seventy-five. There was a pond where you used to build a fire and go skating.

As we grow older we experience the shock of cruelty. We witness as some creature waits to be killed.

> *Back legs*
> *Buckle; it squats*
> *And squirts the snow . . .*

To become a man, the poems say, is to see things as they are. From the height of a scaffolding you see the town where you grew up

> *whole and sadly small*
> *For the first time, bordered by river,*
> *Rusty bridge, and walling hills.*

We have all seen our youth diminished in this way. Poets dedicate themselves to preserving the reality, and where they do not find it they create it themselves,

> *Trying to get the feeling*
> *That will please me*
> *As working construction once did.*

As with Joyce's Stephen Dedalus, the life of the poet and his book grow wings. The consciousness of the poet, having passed through the local, as William Carlos Williams said it must, is *dépaysé*, exiled not only from its native place but from earth itself, like the man in the extraordinary poem, "Hang-glider."

> *Neighbors hate you —wires full of*
> *That tangled, high-pitched whisper*
> *Driving dogs to howl and leap.*

It's not courage, someone tells us, but *la connerie*. Well, maybe so, but "there you are/ In a sky hungry for color, staying up . . ."

On the basis of memory Peter Makuck has built us his world. The poetry is in the building, the use of language, intimate, exact, colorful. Each poem has its own reality, its own unexpected and moving truth.

--Louis Simpson

PART ONE

...the mere sensuous sympathy of dust for dust.
— Nathaniel Hawthorne

Racing

From the A & W drive-in
We'd simmer toward that long dark stretch
Flanked by graveyards
Where even the dead were divided,

Kill our lights and let the dark come in.
We revved up.
Someone signaled with a match.
Tires screamed
And roared for that blind curve at the end.

Win or lose,
We'd be back and back for revenge.
Then as now
We'd burn and squint into that flying dark.

Skating

At the mill, I lived all day
For the pond, for this breath
That lifts like a white thought,

The silence spreading after each car
That cannot stop on the pike
Or anywhere but home or the store.

I gather twigs and deadfall limbs
And walk on cold toes
For mulch in the field, build a pile

Then touch it off.
Trees grow and glide out of the dark.
My skates rumble and scrape.

The ice between ponds
Goes off like a shot of warning
And I guess why no one is here.

From the back pond
By the dumping spot that spills
To the water, I drag an old door

To the flames, praying
They'll come to play tag
And coast between the muskrat mounds.

I tend the fire,
Going into darkness for fuel.
I bring back discarded things

To make it bright
And with my dead friends
Go round and round in dangerous light.

Binoculars

At Midway
My uncle filled them
With kamikazes, boas of smoke, flakpuff
And a sky full of Hollywood flames.

War over,
He gave those heavy tubes to me,
"The little Marine,"
For backyard battles with playmates.

At night,
Hooded like a great hawk,
They perched on my tall bureau
Resting from the hours I would move

What I wanted
In and out of their bright sharp circles,
Then dive for cover, like Uncle, a gunner
Mad for movement, magnification.

Carelessly
I filled them with anything
And envied how they enlarged and then forgot
The choppy lake, stone sky, and how

Uncle fired
Over trees at a formation of ghost fighters
And followed one peeling off, bearing in,
To bang down a mallard.

I watched
Squirrels and pheasants fall in the lenses
And Mrs. Daniels undressing at night
Until my eyeballs throbbed at the root.

At the track
I learned to focus "fillies" in the stands
Then swing the horses, liquified with speed,
Into dark tunnels beating with blood.

Now they dangle,
Twist on a cracked leather strap from a coat-tree,
And stare at the floor for days,
As if in a VA ward, not wanting to focus.

Dziadek

Off Route 44
A dusty road winds back
To an abandoned farm
(Like Dziadek's)
Assaulted by briar and weeds
And going back to the land.

Only highschoolers come out here
To park
And nightly shed their skins
That wither in the dust
Under white July suns.
But I have come to take photos
To find a way of seeing the farm.

When he died
They came from three states,
Dutifully, in winter.
Smoke in the closed car
Burned my eyes
As we waited for the priest
At the graveyard
And my aunt told how he chose
The suit he would wear
And the prayers he wanted said.
The Sobieski Knights,
Men of the same soil,
Shivered, threw sods,
Then left for different farms.

How shall I frame it?
Through blurred daisies and stems?
There must be a way
To capture, to hold the color
Of heat in these fields,
But within me it is black and white
And cold
And snowing past parlor windows
Where Dziadek lies
Yet leads me away
From weeping aunts and drinking uncles
To see the cows that heat the barn
With the heavy raw smell of their bodies
As they stand and chew,
Mouths dangling silver threads of saliva.
Krowa, comes his raspy rattling whisper.
Krowa, I say after him
And touch the rough hair of its face.
My hand winces and he laughs.

I sit deep in clover,
Sight the barn through
Fuzzed, slender reeds of grass.
It leans out of plumb,
Broken-slatted and baring
Its wooden bones to the wind.

Once again, snapped tangent
To the rusty gutted pick-up,
Thin vertical lines of sun
Burn between its shrunken
Dark-grained boards, precisely

Like the barn where I went
To be bitter and alone
Because the priest was late,
Because my eyes still burned,
(But not from smoke)
And the priest had read the wrong prayer.

Krowa, I say as I circle the house.
Krowa, a word that breaks off a bit
Of the farm and Dziadek,
The whisper, the white mustache
And his brown-toothed laugh.
Krowa. The relic of an ethos
I have glimpsed and my children
Will never know.

I am walking through
Shadowy empty rooms,
The walls shaling faded floral paper,
Chunks of plaster and its fine
White dust. Shadows and the hot
Dry smell of rot make a squirm
At the pit of my gut. *Krowa,* I mouth it
Like a prayer.

I come upon a frame of light
And aim through the broken pane
That gives on wild roses, breeze-tossed,
Scratching upon the house.
Now I shoot, the pane out of focus,
And focus on the rose
And suddenly I have found
What is meant by aiming out.

Standing in the knee-deep grass,
I frame the house this one last time
So as not to forget.
I whisper *krowa, dziadek.*
The cows are still chewing
And Dziadek takes my hand.

Holding On

Climbing past shiny black windows
Of coupled neighbors
Toward the Big Bear
Trapped in his usual place,
I barely see
The light from my apartment below.
Friends have left
Empty glasses and dead cigarettes.

When I was seven
They spoke of bigger shoes for my uncle.
The dead feet swell, aunt Mary said.
And that night, I couldn't get down
From the front-yard elm. My father,
A white face with arms and toes, became
Himself as he climbed,
Big as the summer moon,
And held me with a husky whisper,
Taking me down on his back.

Now there is no one below me
No one above,
And I hug the tree as if it were he
Or I were a father

Lowering my son from fear.
But I have no son
And I'm clinging again,
Whispering in a web of branches,
Muscles rigid as wood.

The sky hardens.
Roofpeaks sharpen their edges.
Bark scrapes from under my shoes
Until I find a hold
And think of my father
With all that weight on his back.

Witness

(after a photo in "The Best of Life")

Faces that encircle
The boy and the fox
Encircled a small wood

And moved the game
To this field of snow
Cropped and tense

Black and white
Shaped by an idea
Of time and space —

Holmes County, Ohio,
Where a fox is cornered
Panting on black legs.

The tongue dangles
Like a rag. Back legs
Buckle; it squats

And squirts the snow
With terrified piss.
It does not see

The club, the boy
Hatted like a batter
With a Little League grin.

His last two swings
Have made two foxes
Stiffen on the ground

Like exclamation points
At his feet. No shadows.
The sun is elsewhere.

Family faces, expectant.
Smiles, mute cheers.
They back him.

It is time; he steps
Cautiously forward
Like the crowd's one wish

Cocking his long stick
In this paper place
Of primal black

And white
Where we must gather again
And again.

The Commons

They are changing its look.
A bulldozer pierces its skin,
Noses in a red depression

And mows down trees at the edge.
A crane comes up
With jawfuls of earth, the stump

And dangling roots of an oak —
An image of Saturn
Fisting his half-eaten child.

A rust wind blows at dusk
From the diggings, dirt sifting
Back. There is nothing to help:

In our daydreams
Or the flickerings of deep sleep,
The Commons will never change:

The bell is clanging,
We gather in the sun,
The rifles are about to speak

May 4, 1970
Kent State University

Hunger

Next to his shack, my neighbor hangs
A six-point buck by the hind legs.
It dangles from an apple bough
In this white papery air between us.
I tell him I used to trap
Muskrat, mink, and coon — coon when
All the kids were randy for Crockett hats
And ringtails brought as much money as mink.

Behind his flensing knife,
The beige hide gives way to red meat,
His muddy yard to my father's garage:
A muskrat hangs from a beam, nearly naked,
Its fur pulled inside out
Like a bloody glove on my hand,
Newspaper spread at my feet.
I'm fast; I never make holes in a pelt.

He smiles at me like an old buddy
But a blade is between us, a carcass, and
Something else. Rifles bark in the hills
And he smiles a demented smile as I quicken
Like a dog, stiffen.
At the back of my mind, a cold garage.
A wild season begins and blood-flowers,
One at a time, then clusters,
As if by magic,
Bloom through the newspaper print.

Meat

I
In his old-country beard, your grandfather
Blessed himself, a steaming tub in the background.
You see the barn-beam, the pulley and rope
And the eye-level pig twisting before
That autumn knife shaped like a ritual squeal.

II
The cowpoke squints (his cheek a tumor of tobacco)
And electrically prods the endless steers
Up a wooden ramp to the first specialist
On the disassembly line of this long factory.
They call him "the killer" and, armed with electrodes,
He shocks the bellowing beast to its short knees,
As the metal door flings open and, end over end,
It falls into a hot red light where a hoister
Chains a hindleg and up kicking, wide-eyed and
Upside-down, it takes a clanking overhead tram
To the gum-chewing throat-cutter. See
How he uses the special tool to get that bright
Spurt and spray on rubber boots and apron. See
How the white-suited slitters joke and wait
For bellies while stropping their blades. See

How the cavity-men lean in to unpack that
Hot rank case, root with a sharp right hand
And turn with armfuls of gutflop: lungs and
Liver, kidneys, glands, the still-wincing
Heart, mucus, silver plop and slither. See
How the conveyor men, earphoned against clank and
Roar, watch football in four tubes along the line
And let their hands go down and out and in —
A pattern of cut and lift, sometimes a squint
At the tripe, a wish for the gold watch
That might have been swallowed. But on to the saw-
Men who make the sides (with a high motorized whine),
The skinners, drapers, heavers and haulers, inspectors,
Heapers of hides, boilers of gristle, packers and
Shippers — God loves them all, as He does the ears
And tails, boilings and try-outs, crimson tides,
The drain-suck, the bone, the shit and the bristle.

Workin' Construction

Good hefty words.
Better than mixing mortar
And shouldering the bricks
That made those college summers
Ache for the first two weeks
Or more.

That phrase
Meant money, muscle, a deep tan,
Shots and beers — nothing
Like the light of words
I couldn't find at night, drunk
With fatigue on my parents' back porch,
Fireflies fading
                 one by one
Like bits of the day.

It took me a whole summer to read one thin book.

Mornings, back I went to
Dizzy smells of mortar and firsap,
Cardboard and creosote,
The sight of girders going up and
Welders hunched over violet torches
Binding great steel frames of sky.

By the end of summer
Our brick tiers took us above the town
I saw whole and sadly small
For the first time, bordered by river,
Rusty bridge, and walling hills.

       Below me
It all begs for focus.

          The whistle blows.

The masons snap clean their trowels.
Jaw and joke.

       And hand over hand
I talk myself down to the ache and smell,
Trying to get the feeling
That will please me
As working construction once did.

Lapidary

The sky dims
On two men
Waist-deep
In tilted slabs.
With binoculars
I pull them in
To this dark room
Flatten
The gray woods behind
Blur
The ironweed
To a vague frame.
Air blackens
Like the glass chimney
Of a lantern
About to go out.
Work faster. Shim
And level
In the ink shade
Of cypress.
Small flags
Wilt in the stillness
Lose color
In the gloaming.
Granite clouds
Roll in
Faintly carved
With lost faces
I love.

Rain arrives.
The men flee.
The stone is up
By itself at last
Shining
Saying BROWN
In the rain. Last
It seems first
A pink beginner
At peace.
In the room
In the brown light
My hand
On dark wood
Is carefully chiseled
Glows
Like a white
Piece of stone.

Nights

Next door, he climbs under
A jacked-up Chevy with a droplight.

His girl rags off
The silver tools before passing them under.

Tire-scream and glasspack-rumble.
The concerto in my room goes weak.

But when they quit
It's a black quiet.

I lie down and my mind gets up
In its sleep.

At my kitchen table
He leans over a blank page —

Cut hands and cracked nails
Rimmed with slim moons of dirt.

He is mocking
Up a list of my loves:

The click of well-seated valves,
A good rock beat for the drags,
A girl beside me,
The beautiful poor white girl
Who will litter me kids,
Adjust the light, shadows for make-up.

PART TWO

Living, I want to depart to where I am.
— D. H. Lawrence

Steel Valley

I

A road runs away from the clean blaze
Of mums and lilies   the gold vestments
Of a worn myth   I am trying to understand
To adjust to the city   to inlaws and Sunday visits
While her father drives toward the smouldering mills
A line of tall leaking stacks   a gray breath that rises
To a low sky between the frontseat heads   the opposite hill
Like this one rises squared and cubed
With houses   stained by black rain

I see a kite   green and going up from a space
Between houses   and a boy on a plot of grass
Watching it wiggle past perilous wires

As we glide down the hill   down to the sootblack trestle
Where a train of gondolas heaped with coal
Grates into millcaves   cupped with quivering fire
And emerges with slag   a process of making
The car we ride in   halted by the tracks   the red
Flashing light behind the bluish breath of cars on the bridge
The Mahoning River red as hot steel
The sunstruck welfare windows burn like a furnace
And blacks in the doorways   of boarded stores linger
As if refusing their homes   their slag-gray lives

II

Little cops and robbers near her uncle's home
Chase each other with capguns blazing
And older boys with a football make me itch
To get out of the car   out of myself
For kites in all corners of the city's raw burnt air
Strain at their strings

I am with her uncles and aunts
The room hot and continuous with common talk
Until her uncle shows me   mollies guppies and angels
Coming and going   breeding behind glass   and one
The color of fire   fire that burns and doesn't
And I try to listen   try to love but can't quite
Forget the image of kites
Trying to fly the town from the mills

III

Going home past shoals of men   the day
Shift going   the night shift coming
The sore task that does not split
The Sunday from the week   men who fire the flames
Uncured by the kite   as it wiggles up
Or what wiggles   home in their wives
And screams could shoot off within me
But for the gentle stringtug
That keeps my mind aloft

  The green kite
  Struggles up
  And high on its tether
  It flutters then hangs
  Cruciform   steady
  In the buffeting wind

Deliverance

The overhead mirror holds us in its convex stare.
Now I nearly belong to this monstrous family.
Green rubbery arms and legs, my head bulged —
A last minute fear of the hydrocephalic I'm helping
You squeeze out. You pant. I root for the bright blood
Like a fan. You grunt and cry out and sweat
In the stirrups, the mirror gaze that keeps me
From running off drunk with my buddies. And now
You crush my wrist, giving me pain like a gift
I've needed, wanted, ready at last to be born.

My Son Draws an Apple Tree

I watch it grow
At the end of his dimpled hand
Rooted in white paper.

The strokes are fast
And careless, as if the hand
Had little time.

Quick black trunk,
A green crown and in the white
Air all by itself

A red splotch,
An apple face with a frown
That is his

He gravely says
Looking up at me — the stiffening
Branch he falls from.

Wine Country Near Les Abymes

A gutted Renault, a rust-stained bathtub
For watering cows, flung trash, a privy in the garden —
West Virginia gothic in France.

And between the kind of arbors
I hadn't expected, a sun like raw meat at the end.
No grapes. Black twisted roots.

There is a *cellier* — a door in the hillside
Where men escape wives, rack the guns, gut rabbit,
Let wine rev up their lives.

Vinerows, like the lines of proud poems,
Vanish foot by foot in the dusk. Far off, the Belledonnes —
Peaks that are cold, sharp, killingly pure.

Dépaysé (I)

In the mountains above Chambéry
I found a place, a kind of overlook
With a stone cross
And went there often with my son.

The air was gray, tired.
The car metal ticked as it cooled.
We sat in the lee of a high wall
Away from the wind
But in the full empty sound of it.

The road went back down,
Unspooled like . . .
Comme une espèce de . . .
Nothing,
Not one thing had the right name.

On the wall
The cement covering had cracked,
In places fallen
And left exposed
The skulls of smooth white stones —
Une vingtaine
I counted for something to do.

Now and then

I'd mold a smile for my son.
He sat and hummed
And turned his plastic truck
Through the amber sand
Washed from higher slopes.

The village
Would stay below, far below,
Wordless, sullen
And keep to itself

Dépaysé (II)

Where the wall
At the end
Turned blind
One by one
They appeared
Suddenly making us
Smile, and say *Moutons*
At the same time.
First the bellwether
Bonking and bleating
Then the others
Hundreds
Seeming too heavy
For broomstick legs
Moved

Through a throat
Of stone fence
Into a lower meadow
Followed by
A red-faced shepherd
And two dogs
That kept them
In a changing form;
They flowed
Thick and gray-white
Toward the huddle
Of houses below.
For the first time
My mind moved
Cautiously
In the alps
Of this new tongue:
Les moutons...
Un moutonnement de maisons...
Toits aux tuiles...
Rouge foncé....

Where We Live

In wine country, a postcard village.
Our neighbors are growers
And cut back vines for the spring.

One beats his wife. Today he fell
Drunk from his *vélo*. She picked him up
While we watched

Ourselves: my wild words,
You biting back tears.

Then back to the arbors.
At sunset he was still at it with shears,
Kneeling his way to the row-end.

France wakes from its wine dream.
My hand cramps. Kneecaps ache.
At the edge of the vineyard

Sarments stand in a pyre:
Any night now they will burn.

A Sense of Ending

Uncle, you come around the corner of the shed
In splattered coveralls, not dead, not yet
Falling with the paint pail you threaten

To throw if I cut class to paint and swap tales.
Those rain-pipes, the only thing you left undone,
Lean against the bright white planks of the house

Waiting for a brush. In the fever of this flu-dream
It makes sense to see you in splattered coveralls
Rounding the shed corner, ready with a one-liner,

But even feverless, I've seen you in walks by the river.
A boat passes, waves echo and echo on the bank.
I think of endings, how no ink circle will hold you.

You and I, Uncle, go on with the same fond skits.
Our one-liners rip. Rain-pipes lean. Your pail slips.
A boat passes. Ripples echo and echo on the bank.

Above Challes-les-Eaux

On good Sundays, gliders in slow motion
Tack the cliffs searching for thermals

Then widen the blue between themselves
And the stone chapel of Mont Saint Michel.

Stubby as a bee, the tow-plane groans
To get them aloft. With a few Savoyards

We climb toward the taunting whistle.
The sudden white cross becomes a plane

Barely moving upwind, then skimming
The chapel of the archangel — keeper

Of a bolted dark. Sometimes from behind
They surprise us, drift just overhead

And draw open the deep green space beyond
Our shoetips. We stand and watch

The great wings tilt, the pilots, sealed
In a system of silence, work and work

For that final lift. Now they soar and
Bank, quiet and bright and simple

Like parts of ourselves we have no time
To fly. But here: the steep path,

Rocks, pink thistles, huge whistling wings
And some fragile presence above Challes-les-Eaux.

Hang-glider

. . . Le travail imbecile de chaque jour
— Camus

I saw you, a bright red stain
Blown against the huge cliffs
Behind our house. Excited climbers
From the village gendarmerie
Lowered that broken body, slumped
In a yellow net of nylon rope.

You died all day and night but
Still soar in our marrow and blood.
I see a shadow fly on the snow
Before the hum and high whistle and
Red kite panel slide above us
With a dangle of legs and skis.

You cock back my head with
Another pass, hanging from wires
And nylon-silk, a helmet and
Goggles — no face. You must be
Hiding from your wife. But why?
I've seen her often in the street —

Young, blond, beautiful, looking up
As if your red kite might suddenly
Appear, slowly circling the summit.
But who is it for? This grace-
Ful handling of winds that keeps
The valley from blowing away?

Neighbors hate you — wires full of
That tangled, high-pitched whisper
Driving dogs to howl and leap.
Now it is quiet; the stain is gone.
And I know what to think: no man
With a wife and two children . . .

C'est la connerie . . . not courage.
I know, I know. But there you are
In a sky hungry for color, staying up,
Fabric straining, wires sending
Some inaudible message to dogs
That howl and leap at our fences.

Sleds on the Rue de l'Eglise

Boys fall
One after another
Into the speed of the hill.
Here it's a *luge* — no steering bar,
All wood, even the runners.

Every time down
It gets darker and I hear
Our mothers, yelling from porches.
But these just appear in doorways
Or empty the street
With a wooden clap of the shutters.

I lie down
Stiffly in the cold room, settle
With the snow outside.
My Flexible Flyer whispers
Like sleep on the hill: Benny
Ropes a bumper for the ride back up.
A white space
Widens between us.
House lights come on.
Some mothers yell,
Others just lean for the shutters.

Yet the snow is the same —
Not young or old; it provides
The voice that wakes us, draws us
Shivering to silver windows
To meet the dream of friends
Sliding under streetlamps.

But it's our mothers
Who call
From a great distance,
From varnished doors
Deep under snow.

Driving to Youngstown

Stagnation alert.
Gray shapes on a white scrim.
No day for old men
And I change
The Ohio Valley for an image
Of the Rhône,
Its swollen green muscle at Vienne.

Everything turns
To flowering pear *en espalier,*
Groves of olives
With trunks twisted,
Limbs gnarled,
And silver-green, franc-sized leaves.
Hours pass like Cézannes.

Over the blackened bridge
Past the purging flames of Republic Steel,
I arrive
Leaving behind me
Light slanting
From a hard blue sky
On crenellated walls the color of honey.

Crickets ache.
The suburb steams.
TVs flicker like blue votive lamps.
By midnight
I might be the only one left.
The cathedral gongs. *Platanes* whisper
In the Rue du Château.

The den curtain
Wavers in another tongue.
My body is suited
In coolness at last,
Encircled
Like an alp
In its own weather.

Split

Evening comes down the tree
Limb after blue limb
Like a boy called by his mother.
The house wheezes, dishes crawl in the sink.
The water pump pounds like a bad heart.
Plaster is cracking
Next to the phone — a black growth
That makes me look and look away.
Windows are black and blue
From the back of my hand.
I stare at the bedroom photo, stop,
Listen for a step, a bell to blurt out.
I mix a drink and drink
Until I'm a father again.
Ease open the door, peek
In on the massacred toys, growing dust,
The dark. Snap on a light,
Every light in the house.
Grab Jack Daniels by the neck
And knock back another, kick something
In every room. Laugh like hell. Remember
I'm the guy who takes no shit
From nobody,
Nothing.

A Walkabout

burning instead of beauty
— Isaiah

In the last fires of October
I give my body its own ways.
Rock rhythms from a high window
Beat the space between buildings.

I've been following a girl
With eyes as light blue as her jeans.
Grasshoppers flicker in the weeds
Behind the backstop carved with names.

Three or four rabbits flash their white
On the infield as if on a griddle.
A face in her face. Something more.
Drifting clouds don't understand

The drifting, the moods, a pine
Stiff in its hot black shadows.
Under the bleachers there's a ghost —
A girl in a noose, the kicking shade.

The sun slides a hand on my thigh.
The touch — it's her best souvenir.
But toward home, panic and heat
Are the oldest tokens of absence.

I enter at last by the gate,
By the terrible sweet-burning mums
Guttering toward a winter gray
And everything racked with depth.

PART THREE

Why try to know anything about a place?
— Rudolph Wurlitzer

Pitt County, North Carolina

I
A map of need in back of the eye,
Blue vein and red,
Space for a ten-speed trek,
Hog and tobacco land, want and shadow.

Cross the Tar River Bridge
And sense the boundaries of heart
And lung, mother and father, South
And where I began in the North.

It's panic in a pothole, fear
On this empty back road — something
Like damp earth or dogs lurking
Under cabins on brickwork stilts.

It's a broad field of yellow leaves —
Yellow like the first two fingers
Of my mother's right hand and
Sweat starts from my elbow and chin.

Between corncrib and outhouse,
A washline droops and drags its motley
Flags in the dust. A Nash bakes
In its blistering paint. A hog roots

And I ride off his fat in a setting
I saw years ago from the small door
Of a book. Now I'm here at a barrel
Of rain where a mother does wash.

The shack leans, a tractor bumps
In the ruts. And in the furrows
I meet my thoughts, a whole family
Black and sweaty, resting on hoes.

I pump to a paintless church
Where God spends Saturday night
Honing a radio voice for the hours
Dying in a mother's bedroom.

I spin on, bound to the bike —
The stick-tied leaf they're barning up
For the cure, the sad cure that leads
To nothing but smoke, writhing and

A filling station: Coke and Ice
And a wooden portico sagging artfully
Out of Walker Evans — Let us now praise,
If nothing else, this place of turning.

II
A flat land, and no free rides.
The same way back only darker —
Ash on a pillow, burns on a chair.
And hubtick tightens the dark

Room that develops the pictures
Of Mom and Dad, an old map of the past.
North or South? What does it matter?
It's a tough trek — out and back

Like up and down a hill for nothing.
A bad joke: Calling the tobacco shop
As a kid and asking if the man
Had poor Prince Albert in the can.

Hello, this is no joke. Mom, Dad,
I'm almost home. It's a restless dark.
Those airless rooms. We cough and
Reach; we cough and hack and reach.

Southern Snow

It transforms the street and yard,
Rends us by being rare. Still stiff with sleep,
We watch our son jump off the porch, disappear
Almost with no memory of wet wool, snow
Down the neck. The furnace shivers on.
He dives into a drift, rolls, laughs with a friend.
Does skin touching snow still burn like an angel's?

We are walkers again. Morning's pure resurrection.
Offices closed, we help our neighbors dig out.
We talk. And with no cars to blur the streets
Our listening carries us further than ever.

Tonight more snow. And slowly an unbearable
Sameness. A garage caves in with the weight.
Miz Keel's spotted hand turns brittle pictures
Of the only time this happened before: 1929,
Ford Model A's all mounded high, impounded;
Men in fedoras clown and pose with snowmen
Teaching us how to live with this whiteness
Two more days. Was their laughter really delight?

Weeks from now, at the end of stiff rainy days,
Wild crabtree petals, as a kind of revenge,
Will fill the air, whiten the vigorous grass
And those lost moments will burn again, like snow.

Rerun Scene: You Rescue My Son

The river is fast and black and theatrically high.
Chest-deep, you strain, lean against the current.

You hand me up Keith, dripping and cough-crying
From the fast black river I've climbed from.

I run him breathless to the house, bone-cold, blue,
Hurry him into a hot tub. The skin, numb, stings

Back to feeling. The mud-stink leaves but clings.
The water is fast and black and theatrically high.

We act, minimize to his mother, but all afternoon
He's a little red jacket sweeping down and away.

The TV flickers, booms with a Bowl Game that
Barely reaches the fast black water with heros.

American, cowboy-laconic, we accept the drumming
Of December rain as ironic applause. You lean,

Seem pleased to be straining; you lift him, crying
From the fast black water, giving him back forever,

A sweet mad thanks between us, assumed but unsayable
Except in dreams or rerun scenes like this.

(for Mike)

Teachers

Some odd revolution, Mr. Pasquale, has brought you back
Destroying time and space to get here. It is afternoon

After your lecture on the Era of Revolution and you are
Chewing me out. You remove your glasses, your dark face

Disgusted that I'm merely taking up space, wasting time,
Saying: *Makuck, if breath weren't involuntary, you'd be dead!*

Time, space, and breath. You have none of those now
Except as I give them to you here and watch you get lost

In Revolution, Rochambeau, Metternich, Louis-Philipe, and miss
The revolution of heads in back of the class as our own Philip

Greenwood unzips and brandishes himself in honor of the fallen
Bastille, or something. Laughter brings you back, glasses on,

Angry, toppled. But time, Mr. P., should allow us to laugh
At reversals. This is the Space Age, it's OK to be spacey — look

At this probe to reach you. And my watching the clock's more
Refined, almost an art. But I'm here to praise, not to curse you,

Old teacher, for coming back from an awful nowhere, for no reason
Except, perhaps, to help celebrate ironies and odd revolutions.

Classmates

Maybe once a year my parents fly south for a visit.
At the airport I appraise the hopes that land and
Take off every ten minutes. Then I face them:

The news they have disarms the unfamiliar fields
They cannot notice. That tobacco barn is not
News; but Ellis, my old Little League teammate, is,

Running from a liquor store shot in the back,
Paralyzed for life. That pond of cypress knees
Reflects Bernaki in bed, choked in a wino sleep.

Then at the house, in the yard with a new bottle
Of Early Times, we listen to the leaves, a whispered
Story of the green present, full of shadows at

Hawk and hare, lunging at the greener grass and
The sun turning my mother's hair to unbearable white.
But what's-his-name is a millionaire now.

You know. Skinny kid. Mother divorced and remarried.
He invented an invention for something or other.
I know, I know, and Faulkner invented this phrase:

It's never dead. Gunshots and gagging thrive, a kind
Of happiness against the hedge ringing with crickets.
The azaleas, like cars, come in different colors here.

But Ellis arches his back, the house stiffens, rises
And soars breathless, a white moan, more ghostly
Than swamp gas from its bed of red, red bricks.

Letter Poem

I've been having these flashes
Of your Mom lately: her laugh
The brogue
That lovely laying on of dishes.
I keep seeing you drive
That long drive to Yale New Haven
And wait in the hospital basement
For her suitcase of last things.
It was sadistically light
Wasn't it?

Last night
There were thin pale ghosts of light
Drifting from wall to wall
And I listened to Phyllis breathe,
The faint metal heart
Of my watch tick. Christ
It's frightening — like those bloody, ghastly
Pictures of Christ crucified
The nuns called "holy"
And gave us like poisoned candy.
I thought of how you said that remission
Made summer full
Of ways to show her what had to be shown.
And she knew. This has to be
What grace is
What Christ is
And the nuns never knew.

Once in the middle of the night
Crying
Keith woke up.
I ran to his room.
He hung on tight, sobbed that something
Stinking and black
Was after him in the woods.
It was, is.
And I wanted to get a gun, a chair
And post myself at his door.

Letters like this, my friend,
And poems that fence with death
Are that same thing:
The shotgun aimed at emptiness.
But I'll write anyway
Load both barrels
With words like "love" and "care"
And let it go — a poor poem
Aimed at an emptiness
Active and stinking and black.

(In Memory of Helen Edwards)

Along the Phoenix Canals

The orange, palm, and lemon trees all sprout
Because of them, peek over walls of brick,
Board and adobe, turning toward their source

Or looking at those who have come here for a new
Life of the joints, lungs, heart, and run
Along the high dirt banks, sky at their feet

On the watertop with crowns of royal palms:
Upside-down. The joggers trot, wobble, fling
Themselves to the last houses where the horizon

Produces *braceros* bent over fields of endive.
Endive in December! Staggering as the sight
Of latino faces multiplying at the city's edge.

A doll floats past, face down, as children have.
But the air is dry. Homes never age. Even
Ancient cars look new without their natural rust.

Dogs, junkyard fierce, bark in the patios
Hidden behind high walls that are bright
With firethorn dripping its red on white. Dogs.

The footfalls set them off — a kind of progress
Changing voice from house to house
Where pool-light trembles on the inside walls.

These mild winter mornings, they rise
Early: odd fowl, they beat along the banks
Flapping their arms as if trying to fly from
Reflection, high above the walls of their homes.

Christmas at North Mountain

Just north of Phoenix
A desert place that wants us
To see it:

Ten royal palms,
Ten growing shadows,
Tumbleweed, rocks
And palo verde.

And the overlook peak
With saguaro staggered
Up the slope
As in my favorite western —
The part where nothing happens.

We enjoy it with devilled eggs
And chicken,
Scallions, black olives, and wine.

We toss a football
With Mexican kids
Until the shirt-sleeve air
Turns cold the moment
The overlook peak turns red
With afterglow.

The rocks keep us warm for awhile.
Then the Mexicans leave — their tail-lights
The last warm color.

Now we are gone,
Rolling south under magi stars,
Our bones, pits and crumbs
Already in animal mouths,
Our voices fading from
The tables, palms
And stones.

Jet Lag

From the desert west we jet back east
Where it's already rainy, dark and cold.

We swap the palms for spanish moss.
Home, unpacking, I still see desert

Stars as secondary to the dark,
To parents alone and distant again.

It's bedtime here, time for dinner there:
I can still see mountains in their window —

Old, they survive just fine on their own,
Get plenty of attention from cameras.

When he's sick he doesn't speak and when
He doesn't speak, I'm all alone for days.

My family has settled into sleep upstairs.
By myself, I've never been less alone.

Now I know how the Word can save
And let that gospel word itself in her lap

As always. Altar boys advance in white,
Nuns, priests from an unbelievable parish . . .

I can't sleep — I'm still in a different time.

Turtles

I

Once, near the Great Dismal Swamp
At a Kayo station all draped with velvet tapestries
Of "Jesus Kneeling in the Garden" for $5.98,
I saw two guys out back
Poking a snapper between gulps of beer,
Hooting when its huge hawk-like beak
Fastened to the stick and
Snapped it like a neck.

II

Another time, in the pasture,
A Connecticut autumn, my uncle put a turtle
In my hand, named it, and pointed to the paisley fringe,
Tiny yellow stripes at the neck, underside gold.
On its way to the cowpond, he said, *to hibernate.*

Hi-ber-nate. I heard it exhale
With a melancholy hiss.

He carved my name on the shell.
And the date . . . *because some live to be
Seventy-five . . . no enemies . . . sleep all winter
At the bottom of a pond.*

III

Today, on the way to work:
A moving rock, a slow-poke treat on stumpy legs.
I spin him and step back — a child's trick
That suddenly taunts me with: *hi-ber-nate.*
Here in the South it happens later.

Cars shoot by like projectiles.
He now inches off in his own sweet time,
An inner North
Where my uncle hibernates early.

At the office
All day, faces with names
Steer through a marketplace of others,
Bump, stop, withdraw and move again.
Seventy-five . . . no enemies.
My uncle puts him down and my name turtles off
Selling me to sunlight and ferns, water, lightness, grace —
What he has before his long dark sleep.

Back Roads by Night

A need for it grows — not the white-knuckle stuff
With second-gear rubber, racing for a case of beer,
Dusting some kidface with a hot Chevy. I mean:
That first time I soloed in my father's car
I drove for hours, slowly, through state forest —
A gullet of darkness ribbed out with trees.

A deer sprang from my lights, its tail bouncing
Waving like a handkerchief off in the dark.
Wherever I've lived I've driven at night: beach-
Roads in Maine, waves burning white; one-lane
Bridges, the ridges and hollows of West Virginia.
I've got a letter to mail, I'll say. And slip out.

Glide on back roads where I'll meet no other cars.
Roll by darkened houses, safe as graves, and think
I'm the only one in the whole county awake. Then
Eyes ignite green in my lights. A white tail waves.
One night, in France, in the Alps, a wild boar,
A *sanglier*, stood in the road, all tusk and bristle.

I stopped. White peaks gathered behind him.
He stood there carved by my lights, a mad
And necessary thought, then ran from the road.
I watched him in a small silver field, turn,
Run at the dogs, break through a thicket. Finally
I drove on with those white tusks flashing.

Sometimes, for fun, I'll let a radio preacher yell,
Tell me how easy salvation is, how to "get saved."
It's as simple as the past tense. You only touch
The dial . . . mail in the tithe to Brother Sid.
Tonight what I need is that boar, the magic
Of *sanglier*, a word full of blood; but even

As he breaks thickets in the mind, I see
The pork-butcher, *bon bourgeois,* string him up,
Hang him from an ancient hook in front of his shop.
He turns slowly in the wind and into a small box
Of sawdust under his snout drip the last drops
Of that wild blood, gone, already absorbed.

To the Snow-walker

Space tells matter how to move;
matter tells space how to bend.
— *"Einstein," PBS-TV*

Enough!
That's probably what he said
To our white New England
Street getting whiter
Drifting higher with snow —
Cars useless.

Enough
Of our tall front room
Chilled with gray light
And the window where twigs bobbed
And pointed beyond themselves
For days.

Finally
He told all that white space
To get bent. On foot, into a scourge
Of wind, he hiked toward the hospital
Five miles away, Mom unvisited
For days.

Enough
Of this foolishness, she said
Before he joked about "All for Love"
But meant it. Then the last dark half
Of his ten-mile orbit
The wind strong

Enough
To blow him down by Mr. Donut.
But he reached home, built a fire,
Fell asleep at sixty-eight and
Repeated that orbit for two more
Snowy days.

Enough,
Just enough pride in his voice
To move me longdistance
Here in the sunbelt
Where the only real snow is remembered.
And I wonder is it

Enough
To know the white coming down
On what we do, covering all that matters,
Making us enter the white space and
Bend it with the small dark bodies
Of our words.

Sixty-eight.
Ten miles. Us orbiting each other
In thought like small planets. Snow-walker
Leaning into the white wind —
I can never think of this
Enough.

Players

The yellow ball just clears the net, skids low.
Your racket reaches, flicks and floats it back.

We hit this poem together and watch it shuttle,
Weave against the green of someone else's youth,

The emerald pathos of a dozen different parks.
Back and forth, we build a rhythm, increase the pace,

Then break. With lobs, then steady strokes again,
We stretch our rallies past the average-player five.

We make each other run, lunge to get what is past us,
Play off the impossible. We do anything to outwit

The average, this space that is nothing without us.
Sometimes I take advantage, hit out hard, but you

Still strain for the save, as if it were something rare,
Important as marriage. So the ball leaves yellow lines.

Once, near the ocean, time did a radiant slo-mo.
You raced with your racket extended and the ball towered

To a yellow spot in a sky gone suddenly storm-green;
It hung while you centered in your white dress: white,

Yellow, storm-green, white, the perfect centering.
Too excited, I watched my overhead splash the net.

Then as now, we come together at the net, our faces glad
With sweat, each telling what the other missed, or didn't.

(for Phyllis)

78

Peter Makuck was born in New London, Connecticut, in 1940.
He received a B.A. from Saint Francis College and a Ph.D. from
Kent State University. In 1974-1975 he was a Fulbright Lecturer
on modern American poetry at Université de Savoie, France,
and since 1976 he has taught at East Carolina University where
he is currently Associate Professor of English. *Where We Live* is
Peter Makuck's first collection of poetry; his first collection of
short stories, *Breaking and Entering,* was published in 1981 by
the University of Illinois Press. He currently resides in Green-
ville, North Carolina, with Phyllis Makuck and their son, Keith.

Where We Live has been issued in a first edition of twelve hundred copies, of which six hundred are in paper and five hundred and fifty are in cloth. An additional fifty copies have been specially bound by Gene Eckert in quarter-cloth and French papers over boards: ten copies, numbered I-X and signed, include a poem in holograph by Peter Makuck; twenty-six copies, lettered A-Z, have been signed by Peter Makuck; and fourteen copies, numbered i-xiv and signed by Peter Makuck, have been retained by the publisher for presentation purposes.